THE CRANBERRY BOOK

THE
Cranberry Book

ELIZABETH GEMMING

Illustrated with prints and photographs

COWARD-McCANN, INC. / NEW YORK

PICTURE CREDITS: Page 6, Plimoth Plantation, Plymouth, Massachusetts; pages 9, 17, 20, 33, 37, 39, 40–41, 49, 50, 52–53, 54, 56, and 59, courtesy of Ocean Spray Cranberries, Inc., Plymouth, Massachusetts; pages 12, 22, 25, 35, and 57, small cuts from *An American Dictionary of the English Language,* published in 1864; page 13, courtesy of the Pilgrim Society, Plymouth, Massachusetts; pages 18 and 30, wood engravings made about 1840 by John Warner Barber, original woodblocks owned by the Society for the Preservation of New England Antiquities, Boston; pages 19, 38, 43, and 61 from *Food and Drink: A Pictorial Archive from Nineteenth-Century Sources,* selected by Jim Harter, Dover Publications, Inc., 1980, 2nd rev. ed.; page 25, Elizabeth Gemming; pages 26–27, Timken Art Gallery, San Diego, Putnam Foundation Collection; page 29, courtesy of the Mariners Museum, Newport News, Virginia; page 31, from a nineteenth-century printer's proof book; page 34, Klaus Gemming; page 47, National Gallery of Art, Washington, D.C., Index of American Design.

The author thanks Herbert N. Colcord of Ocean Spray Cranberries, Inc., for his help with cranberry facts and photographs, and Margaret Teel for recipes and advice on cooking and preserving wild cranberries.

FIRST PRINTING

Copyright © 1983 by Elizabeth Gemming

Library of Congress Cataloging in Publication Data
Gemming, Elizabeth.
    The cranberry book.
    Summary: Describes the history of the cranberry, its natural habitat, its botanical relatives and imitators, its cultivation, and its many uses.
    1. Cranberries—Juvenile literature.
2. Cranberries—United States—Juvenile literature.
[1. Cranberries] I. Title.
SB383.G43   1983   634'.76   82-19797
ISBN 0-698-20568-5

Designed by Klaus Gemming, New Haven, Connecticut

Printed in the United States of America

CONTENTS

1 Living Off the Land

Dried fish, hardtack, dried beef, cheese, some oatmeal with suet or molasses once in a while—imagine living for more than three months on such a dull diet! No milk, no vegetables, no salad, no fruit, no eggs, not even fresh water. But that is just what you would have had to eat if you had been a passenger on the *Mayflower,* bound for America in 1620.

The *Mayflower* sailed from Plymouth harbor, England, on September 16, crossed the gray and stormy North Atlantic ocean, and on November 21, after sixty-six days at sea, anchored off what is now Provincetown, Cape Cod, Massachusetts. Pilgrim passengers and crewmen rejoiced, for it had been a rough passage—the little vessel, originally headed for Virginia, had run into dangerous shoals off the "elbow" of the Cape and had turned back to find a safe harbor. A scouting party of Pilgrim men rowed ashore, but decided that the sandy tip of the Cape was too exposed for a permanent settlement. So the *Mayflower* sailed across the bay to what is now Plymouth, arriving on December 26.

By then, everyone on board was yearning for dry land. Capt. John Smith, the famous explorer, had written in his book *A Description of New England* in 1616 that "the herbs and fruits are of many sorts and kinds, as . . . currants, mulberries, vines . . . gooseberries, plums, walnuts, chestnuts, small nuts, etc., pumpkins, gourds, strawberries, beans, peas, and maize." Though it was very late in the year, there might still be a few mellow nuts and half-frozen berries to gather on shore!

The Pilgrims had brought a good supply of provisions from

7

Left: The *Mayflower II,* a modern replica of the Pilgrim vessel.

England to carry them (they hoped) through their first difficult year in their new homeland: brown sugar, oatmeal, raisins, bacon and salt pork, dried beef and fish, butter and cheese, turnips, onions, cabbages, parsnips, jellies and spices, beer, brandy, and lemon juice (that in some mysterious way seemed to prevent the disease scurvy, which caused bleeding gums, loosening teeth, anemia, and weakness). The foodstuffs had been packed in wooden barrels and casks, and during the voyage much of the meat, fish, and cheese spoiled. The Pilgrims faced a long, bitter cold winter, and the first harvest was many months away. To survive, they would have to depend on hunting, fishing, and gathering of whatever wild foods they could find.

Many of these wild foods would be new to the English settlers, and they would have to guess what to do with them—how to eat them and how to cook them. One wild fruit was destined to become an American favorite: the small, sour red berry the Pilgrims called "craneberry" because its drooping, arched blossoms reminded them of the long neck and head of the crane, a well-known bird of Europe.

During that first winter on the Massachusetts coast, the Pilgrims' worst fears came true. More than half of their band of about a hundred sickened and died. They were short of food and tools, and terrified of the native Americans who lived in the forests nearby. They prayed that the Indians would never realize how many of them were already dead, and how many more were weak from hunger and exhausted by grief. They feared the wolves and bears of the dense forest. It seemed as if spring would never come, and to make things even worse, Capt. Christopher Jones of the *Mayflower* was getting his vessel ready to return to England. Soon the Pilgrims would be left alone, as their governor, William Brad-

CRAN·BER·RY (kråń bër e, -bər-e) *n., pl.* **-ries.**
A slender, trailing North American shrub, *Vacci-nium macrocarpon*, growing in damp ground and bearing tart red berries. [Partial translation of Low German *Kraanbere*, "crane-berry" (from the stamens which resemble a beak): *Kraan*, a crane, from Middle Low German *Kran* + BERRY.]

ford, wrote, with "ye mighty ocean . . . to separate them from all ye civill parts of ye world."

Things were not so bad as they seemed, however. One day a man named Samoset approached them. He was a native of the north, and had learned a little English from British sailors in Newfoundland. Another native, Squanto, also befriended the English newcomers. Squanto was a local Indian who had been kidnapped to England and managed to return, only to find his own tribe all dead of a great epidemic.

The Wampanoag tribe, which inhabited some thirty villages in the area, was relatively peaceful. These people had probably lived in the region for a thousand years. Southeastern Massachusetts, which Pilgrim Governor William Bradford called a "hideous and desolate wilderness," actually contained much land that had long been cared for intelligently. The natives lived in inland villages beside streams and rivers in winter, and in spring and summer planted corn, pumpkins, beans, and squashes, even rotating crops on a small scale in the course of their migrations through the woods to the coast.

They also harvested many wild foods throughout the year: wild strawberries in early summer, then raspberries, low-bush and later high-bush blueberries, blackberries, elderberries, and finally, at the height of the golden Massachusetts autumn, the ruby-red wild cranberries of swamp and meadow.

The Wampanoag word for the wild cranberry was *sasemin* (plural *saseminneash*). The Leni-Lenape of New Jersey called it *ibimi* ("bitter berry"). One New Jersey chief, known as Pakimintzen ("cranberry eater") distributed cranberries at tribal feasts and considered them a symbol of peace.

Wild cranberries ripened in such abundance that they were

eaten fresh, ground or mashed with cornmeal and baked into bread, and also stored both fresh in spring water and dried. Indians mixed dried, mashed cranberries with smoked venison (deer meat), fat, and wild onions, boiled the mixture, pounded it to a pulp, formed cakes, and dried them on rocks in the sun. This was pemmican, a survival ration carried on long journeys by natives and later by white settlers. (Pemmican is a cousin of the fancy compressed dried mincemeat in today's supermarkets—and nowhere near as spicy, rich, and sweet.) The Menomini of Wisconsin, where wild cranberries grew in abundance, sweetened them with maple sugar, while eastern Indians mixed the mouth-puckering sour berries with precious wild honey.

Indians dyed rugs and blankets with cranberry juice, and also used cranberries for healing. They made poultices from unripe cranberries, roasted and mashed, to cure scrapes and sores, especially wounds from poisoned arrows. They believed in the berry's special power to calm the nerves. (Today, we know that the cranberry contains a natural antibiotic, and doctors often recommend cranberry juice to people who suffer from bladder infections—for it acidifies the urine and discourages the growth of bacteria.)

During their first spring and summer in New England, the Pilgrims learned a lot from their friend Squanto. He taught them where to look for wild fruits and berries and greens, and where to hunt and fish. He gave them seed corn—in Europe, corn was fed only to cattle!—and taught them to plant corn and beans in the same hills, so the beanstalks could climb up the cornstalk "poles." The Pilgrims also planted their English wheat, barley, and pea seeds, but the European plants did poorly. Meanwhile, Squanto's thirty acres of native maize, beans, pumpkins, and cucumbers did beautifully. It was time for a harvest celebration!

In that life-and-death year of 1621, Governor Bradford proclaimed a day of celebration for all to share. The "First Thanksgiving," a traditional English "Harvest Home" festival, was a three-day cookout, with sports, songs, and games as well as feasting. It was anything but solemn. Ninety native braves arrived with five freshly dressed deer. Pilgrim hunters contributed wild geese and ducks as well as huge wild turkeys. Pilgrim women pounded and stewed and boiled and baked and set out a banquet of cod, bluefish, clams, eels, stewed pumpkin, succotash, leeks and watercress, corn bread, "Indian pudding" (corn meal and molasses), beach plums, purple grapes, and homemade wines.

And was there cranberry sauce to go with the turkey?

No one knows—there is no record of whether or not cranberries were on the table at the first Thanksgiving! If they were, they were most probably baked into cornbread, or cooked together with sweet grapes, or flavored the succotash. Just possibly, they may have appeared as a side dish of English-style preserves, although sugar was extremely scarce. For centuries, northern Europeans had preserved fruit for year-round use as jam and jelly, and they were generally quick to adapt Old World cooking methods to New World foods—the combination of roasted meat (particularly

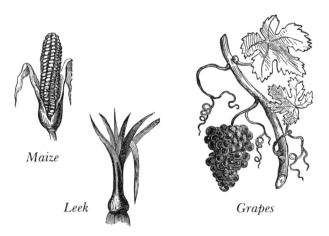

Maize

Leek

Grapes

American Wild Turkey

The First Thanksgiving, a painting by Jennie Brownscombe (1850–1936). "Harvest Home" celebrations were held earlier in the fall than our Thanksgiving, and this picture shows an October landscape, with late wild flowers in the grass and leaves still on the trees. (Some details are not historically accurate: for example, in 1621 the Pilgrims had only rough cottages, not substantial log houses. Also, the Indians of the eastern woodlands did not wear Western-style feather "bonnets," and the Pilgrims' clothing may well have been plainer than the painting depicts.)

strong-flavored wild game and fowl) with the tangy taste of cranberry "sauce" was a natural one. The English may have recognized the North American wild cranberry as a cousin of the northern European lingonberry.

French explorers, too, seem to have been intrigued by the wild cranberry. Samuel de Champlain, who explored the coast of North America from Nova Scotia to Martha's Vineyard in 1605–1608, saw on an island off the coast of Maine "so many red currants that one sees for the most part nothing else." Currants are red, smooth, and round, but not native to Maine, and it is likely that Champlain was describing tiny wild cranberries, which are still plentiful there.

Another Frenchman, Marc Lescarbot, visiting what is now Nova Scotia at about the same time, mentioned "certain small fruits like to small apples, whereof we made marmalade for to eate after meat."

The Englishman John Josselyn visited New England twice during the 1600s and later published a botanical description of the region. He listed:

Sauce for the Pilgrims—Cranberry or Bearberry (because the Bears use much to feed upon them) is a small trayling plant that grows in salt marshes that are overgrown with moss. The berries are a pale yellow color, afterwards red, as big as a cherry, some perfectly round, others oval, all of them hollow with sower [sour] astringent taste; they are ripe in August and September.

Josselyn further noted that "the Indians and English use them much, boyling them with sugar for Sauce to eat with their meat; and it is a delicate Sauce, especially for Roasted Mutton. Some make tarts with them as with Goose Berries."

In England, these delicious berries from America were soon considered such a delicacy and so much better than the English variety that Colonial settlers began exporting them. Shipped back to Europe in barrels of spring water, the berries kept many months without spoiling. In 1677, New Englanders sent ten barrels of Massachusetts cranberries (along with two hogsheads of cracked

14

Indian corn and three thousand codfish!) to King Charles II of England as a gift.

By this time, many shiploads of new settlers had arrived, spreading outward from Plymouth and onto Cape Cod, founding many new towns. All over the Cape, they discovered their favorite cranberry growing wild. An old folk tale tells how it got there:

One day, the Reverend Richard Bourne of Sandwich, a Christian missionary and lifelong friend of the Indians, got into an argument with an Indian "medicine man." The Indian lost his temper and cast a spell on the minister, sinking his feet in quicksand in a bog so he could not move. The two men then agreed to a contest of wits, with questions and answers and riddles. It went on for fifteen days without a winner. Bourne was saved from thirst and hunger by a mysterious white dove that flew to him from time to time and placed a juicy red "cherry" in his mouth. Try as he might, the Indian could not drive the dove away. Finally, exhausted and starving, the Indian fainted and fell to the ground, and Bourne was set free. Meanwhile, one red berry had dropped into the bog, where it took root and began to grow—

And that is how the cranberry came to Cape Cod, where the story of cranberries begins.

2 Cranberries: "Bog Rubies"

Cranberries grow in fields traditionally known as "bogs," but they are not, in fact, true bogs. The word "bog" comes from old Irish words meaning "soft, tender, moist"—yet a cranberry "bog" must be dry during the growing season.

Cranberry plants under cultivation have very definite needs: a firm base of acid soil or peat, a dependable supply of fresh water, and a good source of sand. They like a fairly long growing season without severe frosts—the ocean-tempered climate of Cape Cod is ideal. (Southern New Jersey, Wisconsin, and the Pacific Northwest are also well suited to cranberry cultivation.) Not every cranberry bog today was formerly a natural swamp, but many natural wet bogs have been drained and channeled for cranberry growing.

A true bog, wet and spongy, is a special kind of lake without an inlet or outlet. It has become gradually clogged with water-loving plants such as heath and sphagnum, or peat moss. These plants begin to grow around the edges of open water and slowly form a dense mat in which other bog plants, such as orchids, gain a toehold. Humus (decomposed organic matter) and porous acid soil are built up. It is not the incidental wetness of an ancient bog that the cranberry needs, but rather this peaty acid soil.

Peat is an early stage in the formation of coal and a valuable storehouse of solar energy trapped in the remains of plants. A brown, tightly tangled mass, peat was used as fireplace fuel in coastal New England during the late 1700s and early 1800s. It was dug out of the swamps, cut into bricks, and sun-dried.

16

Cross section of a cranberry bog,
showing layers of peat and sand.

The peat swamps of southeastern New England were formed by a glacier, which is a mass of ice created by the unmelted snows of many winters. It moves forward very slowly under its own tremendous weight.

The Great Ice Age of the Pleistocene Epoch in the earth's history produced at least four glaciers. Geologically speaking, Cape Cod and the offshore islands of Nantucket and Martha's Vineyard are very young, for they were formed during the last advance and retreat of this ice, not more than 25,000 years ago. The last ice sheet probably began to shrink and melt rapidly about 15,500 years ago, leaving a ragged version of today's Cape to be shaped and reshaped forever by winds and ocean currents.

This Cape, a crooked, bent "arm" of land, consists of sand, gravel, silt, clay, and boulders, with no solid bedrock until perhaps 200 to 600 feet below the surface. The land cover consists of rock debris from the ice sheet, called "drift." Wherever the ice sheet stopped, it dumped a ridge of drift, called a "moraine." Most of Cape Cod is drift in the form of "outwash plains," broad, sloping deposits of gravel and coarse sand that poured out of the ice in meltwater streams. (Nantucketers call their plain "the moors," while Martha's Vineyard people call it "the great plains.")

View of Chatham, Cape Cod, with "kettle" ponds.

As the last great ice sheet shrank back toward the north, gigantic blocks of stagnant ice broke off and were left behind, half covered with debris. When these solitary ice blocks melted in time, they caused cave-ins. These roundish cavities are called "kettles" or "kettle holes" and can be wet or dry. Wet kettles are like large open

18

wells of clear, fresh water. Their water supply is regulated by evaporation versus additions from underground springs and rainfall. Many of them, even some very small ones, are popularly known as "no-bottom ponds," for they can be as much as 100 feet deep, underlain by a layer of clay. Dry kettles resemble abrupt valleys, as described by the American writer Henry David Thoreau in his book *Cape Cod* (published in 1865): "Some of the valleys . . . are circular, a hundred feet deep, without any outlet, as if the Cape had sunk in those places, or its sands had run out."

The wild cranberry, native to this heath landscape, belongs to *Ericaceae*, a family of plants, mainly evergreen shrubs, that love acid soil. These plants are the typical vegetation of open moors, damp, low-lying areas, and mountain slopes of temperate regions worldwide. Besides the cranberry, the Heath family includes the blueberry, bearberry, heather, andromeda, wintergreen, rhododendron, azalea, trailing arbutus, and mountain laurel (not a true laurel).

The wild cranberry, like its very close cousin the blueberry, is a creeper of the genus *Vaccinium*. It has smooth hairless leaves, pretty flowers, and round or oblong fruit that is edible raw or cooked.

The blueberry, a very close relative of the cranberry and, with the large wild cranberry and the Concord grape, one of three fruits native to North America.

Cranberry blossoms in three stages: in bud (bottom right), in full bloom
(top right and top left), and after peak blooming (center background).

Vaccinium macrocarpon is the Large, or American, Cranberry. It
is one of only three fruits native to North America, the others being
the blueberry and the Concord grape. It is the only variety of wild
cranberry that has ever been successfully cultivated. Its evergreen
leaves, $1/4$ to $5/8$ in. (1-2 cm.) long, are blunt-tipped, wedge-shaped
to round, flat (or with slightly rolled edges), and pale underneath.

20

Its slender stems grow to 4 feet (1.2 m.) in length with runners to 3 ft. (1 m.) in any direction. Small pinkish-white nodding flowers bloom from late June into August. The vines bear shiny red or dark red berries, 7/16 to 13/16 in. (1-2 cm.) across, with firm white flesh, tiny seeds, and a very acid taste. The Large Cranberry grows wild in boggy places from Newfoundland, western Ontario, and Minnesota to Long Island, in uplands south to North Carolina and Virginia, Ohio, Illinois, and Arkansas. Its berries are eaten by several songbirds, bobwhite, mourning dove, and ruffed grouse (known in New England as "partridge," in the midwest as "pheasant," and in New Jersey as "pine pheasant").

Vaccinium oxycoccus, the Small Cranberry, is found in northern Europe, northern Asia, and North America. Also known as moss berry, moor berry, and bogberry, it is a dwarf shrub that grows to a height of 1 ft. (0.3 m.). Its leaves are less than 3/8 in. (1 cm.) long, egg-shaped and pointed, white underneath with rolled edges. Its stems are very slender. Its pink flowers appear from May to July, and it bears fruit from August to October. The berries, less than 3/8 in. (1 cm.) long, are red or dark red, globular or pear-shaped. In the Western Hemisphere, the Small Cranberry is found in Greenland, Labrador, Alaska, south to Newfoundland, New Jersey, Pennsylvania, the mountains of West Virginia, Virginia, North Carolina, northern Ohio, Michigan, Minnesota, Saskatchewan, and Oregon. It is eaten by grouse, pheasants, and chipmunks.

Vaccinium vitis-idaea, a creeping, mat-forming shrub, is a low-bush cranberry of northern Europe and Asia. A variant, *V. vitis-idaea minus,* native to Canada and the northeastern United States, is known as the Northern Mountain Cranberry. It grows to a height of 8 to 10 in. (20-25 cm.) and has slender stems. Its leaves, 1/4 to 3/4 in. (1-2 cm.), are evergreen and egg-shaped, and are dotted with tiny black points on the undersides. They are crowded on creeping stems. In June and July it has white or pink flowers that are small, bell-shaped, and nod in terminal clusters. The berries, ripe from August to October, are tiny, red, and globe-shaped. The Northern Mountain Cranberry is picked in large quantities in Nova Scotia. It is found in rocky areas and bogs from sub-Arctic Alaska south to Newfoundland, New England, southwestern Ontario, northern Minnesota, Manitoba, Washington, Oregon, and British Columbia. This cranberry is also known in various localities as partridgeberry, cowberry, and wolfberry. *V. vitis-idaea* is known in England as lingonberry, in Scandinavia as *tyttebaer,* and in Germany as *Preisselbeere.* Stewed with sugar, these delicious tiny cranberries are popular in Europe as a relish with roast meat, and they are the traditional filling for "Swedish pancakes" (crepes).

The wild cranberry is often confused with the bearberry of higher, upland sandy areas of Cape Cod. That berry, cottony-tasting and dry, is called by many Cape Codders "hog cranberry."

Two North American plants commonly considered to be cranberries are not. The so-called Southern Mountain Cranberry *(Vaccinium erythrocarpum)* is really a very acid, red blueberry. It stands up to 8 ft. (2.5 m.) tall—true cranberries creep along the ground.

The so-called Highbush Cranberry *(Viburnum trilobum),* also known as Cranberry Viburnum, is not even related to the cranberries. However, some people do use its autumn fruits, which are red and tart, as cranberry substitutes.

Ruffed Grouse

3 "Red Gold"

Most of the early settlers of coastal Massachusetts had come from the island nation of Britain, and their heritage naturally attracted them to seafaring, shipbuilding, fishing, and trading. But every man also had to become a farmer, if only to feed his family. Pilgrims and later colonists were careful to protect many wild foods the Indians had taught them to use, too.

Regulations concerning the rights of individuals to pick wild cranberries were quite strict, especially cranberries on public lands such as the Province Lands at the tip of Cape Cod—these lands were set apart for conservation by the Pilgrims in 1670. No harvesting was allowed until fruit was fully ripe. Provincetown passed a law in 1773 that read: "Any person . . . found getting cranberys before ye twentyeth of September exceeding one quart should be liable to pay one dollar and have the berys taken away."

Wild cranberries also grew plentifully in sandy southern New Jersey, where a 1789 law prohibited picking before October tenth, subject to a ten-shilling fine. In Wisconsin, too, Indians and whites alike set rules so that everyone could share in the harvest of nature. At one time, a penalty of fifty dollars was imposed on any person caught picking or possessing unripe cranberries before September 20. In many native communities, chiefs proclaimed a special day for harvesting. "Cranberry Day," a town holiday and cookout, was held into modern times in the Indian village of Gay Head on Martha's Vineyard island, where there are still many wild cranberries on the common lands. In both cultures, children did much of the gathering of fruits, berries, and nuts.

In the year 1816, Capt. Henry Hall, a farmer-fisherman-saltmaker of East Dennis, Cape Cod, made an historic discovery. He observed that certain wild cranberry vines that were near enough to the dunes to be blanketed by windblown sand seemed not to suffocate, but actually to produce larger and juicier berries than other vines. He also successfully transplanted to another bog some vines from a marsh that produced extra-fine fruit—thus making the first attempt to cultivate and improve the quality of the cranberry. Some people laughed, but soon, sanding became a standard practice and set off a rush to plant cranberries instead of simply gathering them in the wild. The cultivation of cranberries would turn out to be more important to the Cape's shaky economy than anyone realized.

The Cape, a sandspit of low hills covered with scrub pine, has no mineral resources to speak of, no timber trees, no large rivers, and no deepwater harbors other than Provincetown's. In the early to middle 1800s it suffered several severe blows that finally resulted in a great depression. Fish prices fell, and commercial fishing shifted away from Cape Cod towns to Gloucester, north of Boston, as fishermen went out in larger, more modern vessels. Shipbuilding also declined. The railroad—the exciting "iron horse"—came to New England in the 1840s and took over the shipment of goods to the West. The Cape's fleet of small, swift packet boats was no longer needed, and once more, Cape folks had to hustle and scrounge to survive.

The one bright spot in the Cape's sagging economy turned out to be the cranberry! At first, cranberries had been grown for home consumption. But Cape Codders were quick to see that profits from the sale of cranberries could be enormous—and the cranberry boom was on. Prices of bogland soared as dozens of people

CAPE COD

Province Lands

Provincetown

Hanson

Plymouth

Carver

Cape Cod Bay

Wareham

Sandwich

Dennis

Barnstable

Harwich

Chatham

Nantucket Sound

turned to farming "red gold." Many were former sea captains and fishermen who sniffed profits in cranberries as they had once smelled whales and cod in the ocean. Mucky wasteland that no one had cared about for years was suddenly snapped up, cleared, ditched, and planted with cranberry vines. (To this day, Cape Cod and Plymouth County dominate the cranberry industry, seldom if ever losing their early lead.)

The Cranberry Harvest, Island of Nantucket,
a painting by Eastman Johnson (1824–1906).

The town of Harwich, which in the mid-1700s had one of the Cape's largest fishing fleets, is the site of the first (and still producing) commercial cranberry bog in the world. It is former sea captain Alvin Cahoon's old bog on Route 124 north of the modern Mid-Cape Highway. It was built in 1846. For more than a hundred years, the Harwich-Dennis cranberry industry was carried on by former sea captains as well known in Canton and Honolulu as at home on the Cape.

Bog building was expensive and required a good-sized initial investment of time and money. Retired sea captains (and they tended to retire as young as forty, having first been to sea in their teens) often financed their bog acreage the way they had paid for their ships: by selling 1/64th shares. To this day there are bogs on Cape Cod that are co-owned by a number of individuals whose shares have been inherited from ancestors who bought "64ths" more than a century ago.

In the early days, bogs were cared for by family members. The men cleared the land and sanded it, and the women set out the plants and weeded. A five-acre bog was more than ample for a family, which generally had some berries left over to sell. A ten-acre bog enabled a family to live quite comfortably on the profits from the sale of the fruit.

Green carpets in spring, the flat bogs appeared lightly dusted with tiny pinkish-white flowers in late June or early July. Only in the fall did they glow with color—wine-red and bronze leaves and brilliant ruby-red berries. At harvest time, entire towns turned out to pick the berries by hand. Dressed in aprons, coveralls, and sunbonnets, people inched forward on their knees to gather the fruit row by row. They wrapped their fingers with strips of linen for protection against cuts and scratches, and shielded their knees with oilcloth patches on their aprons. It was hard work but festive too. People took picnic lunches and bottles of tea to the bogs, and over the years it became traditional for children to receive special cranberry recesses from school to help pick the fruit.

In the early to mid-1800s, in the heyday of the China trade and of whaling voyages that lasted three or four years, hundreds of American ships carried barrels of cranberries preserved in spring water to protect crewmen against scurvy. We now know that scurvy

Portrait of a sailor, scratched on a whale's tooth. His clothes were patched and ragged after months or years at sea, and he probably received a regular ration of cranberries to supplement his meager shipboard diet. (This is an example of "scrimshaw," the unique folk art of whalemen, who handcrafted articles from whales' teeth and whalebone to pass the time on long, boring voyages.)

ABLE SEAMAN

is caused by a deficiency of vitamin C, which cannot be stored in the body. Cranberries, a good source of vitamin C that kept fresh for up to two years, proved to be the American scurvy preventive, just as West Indies limes became the British navy's favorite.

Massachusetts cranberries continued to be exported to Europe. One Boston food broker who had arranged to ship a selection of fancy foods abroad wrote to the ship's captain (whose job it was to sell the foods at the best price he could obtain):

> Enclosed you have invoice of pickles, sauces, mustards and preserves of first quality. ... The cranberries in the bottles are preserved without sugar. I name this because should any person purchase them for sweetmeats they would be disappointed. They are to be used precisely as if purchased fresh from the market, and will keep any length of time before the cork is drawn. Any English people will understand them, and they will be very agreeable for any American families who wish for cranberry sauce. The cranberry jam is a sweetmeat and usually brings a high price; I have frequently sold it in India for $1.50 per jar.

The busy harbor at Fairhaven, Massachusetts.

Masthead of a Cape Cod newspaper.

In 1856 the Reverend Benjamin Eastwood published an excellent book entitled *The Complete Manual for the Cultivation of the Cranberry.* He declared: "The American cranberry is coming into notice in Europe, but most especially in England. It is sold there in small bottles into which the fruit is first put, and then filled with water and hermetically sealed. We have seen 'Cape Cod Bell Cranberry' sold at four shillings sterling in the Strand, London."

Eastwood was referring to one of the three staple varieties of cranberries grown up to the time of the Civil War: the "Bell," which was pear-shaped; the "Cherry," a round berry; and the "Bugle," oval and pointed at both ends.

After the Civil War, which destroyed the economy of the American South and shook the entire nation, the cranberry, virtually alone, kept Cape Cod from near-certain economic collapse.

Baby tree swallow in its birdhouse at a cranberry bog.

Some growers set up birdhouses on tall poles to encourage tree swallows to nest at the bog: a natural method of pest control. The birds catch insects on the wing, and eat their weight in insects every day. With perfect timing, they return from the South for the spring growing season, and soon need lots of food for their babies. Hives of bees are often rented or borrowed and set up along the edges of the bogs, too. Bees help to pollinate the blossoms and thus increase the yield of the bog. (Beekeepers are glad to loan beehives, because cranberry-blossom honey is sweet and fragrant.) In June and July, helicopters are sometimes used to dust the bogs with insecticides to kill leaf-eating pests, but whatever is used must be nonpoisonous to swallows and bees.

Brief flooding from time to time helps control pests in very dry weather. During the growing season, however, flooding for more than twenty-four hours at a time will damage the vines. If a sudden frost is forecast, bogs must be flooded immediately to insulate the vines against the freeze.

Once the cranberries are harvested and pruning is done, it is time to flood the bog for the winter. "Ice in the bog" usually appears in very late fall and signals season's end. Flooding protects the plants against the effects of cold, drying winds and storms. Every three years or so, an additional half-inch of sand is spread over the ice—when the ice melts in the spring, the sand will fall evenly among the vines, helping to anchor them and encouraging new uprights to reach towards the sunlight. Mist and vapor from the ice cover rise and envelop the bog. And so the bog, purplish under its cover, rests through the winter.

Working Bee

5 A Year-Round Treat

The cranberry boom that had begun on Cape Cod soon spread to Plymouth County. The first official cranberry census was taken by the Massachusetts Department of Agriculture in the mid-1850s, and counted 197 acres on Cape Cod under cranberry cultivation, with the town of Dennis leading at 50 acres. By 1865, there were 1074 acres, with Harwich taking over the lead at 209 acres of cranberry bogs. About 1890, Plymouth County surpassed the Cape in cranberry production, and it still holds the lead. This "inland" region has ideal soil and water conditions for cranberries, especially around Carver, Wareham, Middleborough, and the town of Plymouth itself. While Cape Cod bogs always tended to be small—from ½ acre to about 60 acres, Plymouth County bogs were a bit larger—from 1 to 200 acres.

Through the years, however, the association between the cranberry and Cape Cod remained firmly established. Even though the cranberry was by then being grown in New Jersey and Wisconsin as well, the "Cape Cod ruby" seemed to be forever linked in people's minds with the sand dunes and salt sea spray of the Atlantic shore!

In the summer of 1888 in the town of Sandwich, the Cape Cod Cranberry Growers' Association held its first meeting. Its members numbered about forty growers from Barnstable (Cape Cod) County and Plymouth County. The 1893 crop totaled 575,000 barrels, soon to be surpassed by the 1899 crop, 600,000 barrels. Though the industry continued to use the old-fashioned "barrel" holding 100 pounds as its unit of measurement, it had clearly become a major modern business.

"Combing" cranberries from the vines, which lie close to
the soil. Although wooden scoops may still be used
here and there, most people think of them as antiques.

In the years following 1900, Massachusetts growers worked
seriously to eradicate cranberry pests. Their efforts resulted in the
establishment of the Cranberry Experiment Station in Wareham,
in 1910. There were improvements in bog management, and the
Wareham station developed controls for the disease known as
"false blossom," believed to have been imported from Wisconsin,
where cranberries were also being actively cultivated. A Frost
Warning Service was also established. This service enabled farmers
as early as noon of the preceding day to flood their bogs and save
their crops.

The beloved Cape Cod writer Joseph C. Lincoln, in *Cape Cod
Yesterdays,* described the pleasant local scene:

37

Cranberries and cranberry swamps—or bogs, if you like . . . are almost as common on the Cape as potato patches. . . . In the winter their flooded, frozen surfaces make good, outdoor skating rinks; in the spring their expanse of glistening vines are like great carpets spread in the hollows; in the summer the billions of tiny young berries are showing . . . ; in the autumn is the culmination—profit or disappointment—for the fall is picking time.

If it had remained short-term and seasonal, however, the cranberry industry could never have become the solid business it is today. People could consume only so many fresh cranberries during the harvest and winter holidays, and a way had to be found to process and preserve the fruit so it could be marketed all year round.

Old-fashioned canning jars.

Housewives had been canning cranberries at home, of course, ever since white sugar had become inexpensive enough for everyday use, in the latter half of the 1800s. One Providence, Rhode Island man took out an early patent in food preservation in 1862, packed cranberries in water in sealed jars, and offered them for sale. The first commercial cranberry cannery opened in Wareham, Massachusetts, in 1898. This small-scale operation put up cranberry syrup and jam in glass jars, and it did well enough, but went out of business in 1901.

The Central Packing House at Hanson, Massachusetts, about 1912.
The old Hanson plant was the headquarters of Ocean Spray Cranberries,
Inc., for many years.

In the year 1912, there were 26,300 acres of cranberries under cultivation in Massachusetts, and the harvest that year amounted to 512,000 barrels. Tons of cranberries were on the verge of rotting for lack of a market. This greatly disturbed Marcus L. Urann, a young Boston lawyer who was also president of the United Cape Cod Cranberry Company, of South Hanson, in Plymouth County. He attacked the problem and devised a successful solution: canned cranberry sauce! In 1912, such modern convenience foods were all but unknown, and Mr. Urann insisted that the sauce taste "like homemade." He helped stir up the first batch in a small plant in South Hanson, designed a label, and went on the road to sell his new product, to which he gave the brand name "Ocean Spray," in

Early label for canned cranberry sauce, from the 1930s.

honor of the salt spray that misted the bogs of the Cape. Before long, he was packing 5000 cases of cranberry sauce a year.

After World War I, several other companies began canning cranberries, among them the A. D. Makepeace Co. of Wareham, Massachusetts, and Cranberry Products Company of New Egypt, New Jersey. (The Jersey "Pine Barrens" was another early center of cranberry growing.) In 1930, these two companies decided to merge with the United Cape Cod Cranberry Company to form a cranberry growers' cooperative. Their four canneries in the two

40

OCEAN SPRAY BRAND

Cranberries contain iron, iodine, lime, manganese and Vitamin C.

Cranberries are the product of rich peat soils, warm sunshine, ocean breezes, heavy dews, cool nights and the tinge of fall frost in the ripening season.

The place and time to pack cranberries is where they grow and while they are still fresh.

Berries for this sauce are specially ripened and cured to develop and retain their rich delicate qualities. They are not touched by hand but are carefully cleaned, and scientifically canned with granulated sugar.

Spread on bread for school children. Use it in pies, layer cakes and for puddings, as well as a relish.

Cranberry shortcake—bake your regular shortcake or biscuit batter. While hot, split and butter freely. Spread between and on top Ocean Spray Brand Cranberry Sauce. Add whipped cream if desired. A delicious and easily prepared dessert or luncheon.

Open the can and serve—its ready.

1931

CRANBERRY SAUCE
WHOLE FRUIT SWEETENED - READY TO SERVE

states became the property of the farmer-members. The cooperative chose the name "Cranberry Canners, Inc." but kept the brand name "Ocean Spray." An early label urged housewives: "Always serve Cranberry Sauce with chicken, fowl, and turkey, however prepared" and advertised "ECONOMY—No work—No waste—No worry" and "CONVENIENCE—Skins removed. Ready to serve."

In 1940 and 1941, growers in Wisconsin (already a major cranberry producer), Washington, and Oregon joined the cooperative, which proudly changed its name in 1946 to National Cranberry Association. In 1959, it adopted the name it bears today, Ocean Spray Cranberries, Inc. The cooperative now has about 735 farmer-members in the five states and in British Columbia and Quebec, Canada. More than 85 percent of U.S. growers are members. (A typical non-member cranberry grower may own a small family-run bog and sell his entire crop locally.)

The cooperative is unusual among food companies because those who own it are themselves directly involved in production and marketing. They are not merely stockholders who invest money. It is wholly and directly owned by independent farmers, who deliver their freshly harvested cranberries to one of the cooperative's processing plants and receive processing and marketing services in return. There are plants at Bordentown, New Jersey; Kenosha, Wisconsin; Markham, Washington; and Middleborough, Massachusetts. The Middleborough plant, finished in 1976, is longer than four football fields—481,729 square feet in area, and is capable of turning out 4½ million cases of cranberry products a year.

The cooperative system aims to ensure a proper return to all members for their labor, and profits after expenses are paid are shared by the members. It also strives to provide consumers with attractive, high-quality products at a fair price. In the more than fifty years of the cooperative's existence, the growers, by pooling their resources, have created new markets for cranberries at home and in more than fifty foreign countries, bred new varieties of fruit, and developed better harvesting methods.

In 1959, the thriving cranberry industry suffered a devastating shock. Just before Thanksgiving, Arthur Flemming, then United States Secretary of Health, Education, and Welfare, announced that some cranberries grown in Washington and Oregon were contaminated by a herbicide (weed killer) that caused cancer in laboratory rats. The Department of Agriculture had actually approved the experimental compound, Amino Triazole, but HEW reversed that decision. One of the first sensational cancer scares hit the headlines.

That year a near-record crop of cranberries had just been combed from the bogs, in time for the holidays. There were no reports of contamination from the far more important cranberry states of Massachusetts, Wisconsin, and New Jersey, yet the entire crop was suspect. Overnight, the price of Cape Cod berries fell from $13 to $3 a barrel. The Secretary of Agriculture, Ezra Taft Benson, announced that he, for one, was going to go ahead and eat cranberry sauce with his Thanksgiving turkey anyway. But many people panicked. Grocers everywhere took cranberry sauce and juice and fresh berries from their shelves, and restaurants crossed cranberries off their menus.

The following March, the government agreed to a $10 million subsidy to cranberry growers for unsold berries free from contamination. It confirmed that only a tiny part of the national crop had ever been treated with Amino Triazole, and the weed killer was eventually declared to be harmless to humans by the University of Massachusetts Cranberry Experiment Station. Nonetheless, no cranberry grower would ever think of using it again.

Cock Turkey

43

6 Cranberries, Coast to Coast

 Today, as you might expect, Massachusetts is the leading cranberry state, with 40 to 45 percent of the annual crop. Cape Cod produces about 10 percent of this crop. Most bogs are located in the southeastern part of the state; more than half of the state's approximately 11,000 acres (1980) are in Wareham, Carver, Plymouth, Middleborough, and neighboring towns. Many bogs are adjacent to residential areas. Most of these bogs are situated on ancient peat swamps and are relatively small, producing fewer than 100 barrels a year. The average yield per acre is about 105 barrels.

Wisconsin is the second-largest cranberry producer, accounting for 35 to 40 percent of the U.S. crop. Some 7000 acres of cranberry bogs are spread over a vast area of the state—in the marshy sections of the southwest, in the northwest, and in the northernmost woods. Bogs here cover wide expanses, unlike the scattered bogs of Massachusetts.

Cranberries grew wild in Wisconsin long before they were first cultivated in 1853 near the town of Berlin. By 1865, 1000 acres of improved marshes were under cranberry cultivation and the industry was well established. Cranberry-growing areas of Wisconsin also produce mint, sphagnum moss, and sunflowers. About 80 percent of the state's growers produce more than 1000 barrels a year. Yields are high, averaging about 150 barrels per acre.

In recent years, New Jersey has been the third cranberry state, with nearly 10 percent of the national total. Most cranberries are grown in the Pine Barrens, a 1¼-million-acre region in the south-

44

central part of the state. It is a region of dwarf forests of scrub oak and pitch pine, fern, wild orchids, and blueberry bushes by the millions. (The jumbo hybrid cultivated blueberry was developed in the Pine Barrens early in this century.) Unlike Cape Cod, the Pine Barrens was not covered by the last great ice sheet, which halted about fifty miles to the north. But torrents of meltwater from the ice carried out tons of gravel that mounded here and there to form hills. Great cedars took root, grew tall, and eventually died and crashed to earth to rot and remain preserved in ponds as spongy sphagnum, or peat moss. Of New Jersey's more than 3000 acres of cranberry bogs, the largest concentration is around the town of Chatsworth. Cultivation began in 1825, when Benjamin Thomas built a bog near Pemberton. New Jersey growers average about 85 barrels per acre.

Out in the Pacific Northwest, cranberries had long played an important part in the diet of natives and newcomers alike. In the winter of 1805-06, the explorers Lewis and Clark had purchased wild cranberries from the Indians of the Oregon territory. Later in the 1800s, Oregon pioneers had gathered cranberries both to eat and to ship to logging and mining camps as far away as California—the vitamin-deficiency disease scurvy was as much a problem in isolated inland settlements as it was on ships at sea.

Today, the state of Washington usually accounts for about 5 percent of the total crop. Its major cranberry-growing areas are all near the coast. There are nearly 1200 acres of bogs in all, most near Grayland. There are also many on the Long Beach peninsula, where the cranberry was first cultivated in 1883 by Anthony Chabot, with vines brought from Cape Cod. Washington bogs are rather small, but yields are normally more than 120 barrels per acre.

Nearly all of Oregon's approximately 900 acres of bogs are in the southwestern part of the state. Oregon produces about 3 percent of the total crop. Some Oregon bogs are interestingly constructed of terraces of three or four levels. This conserves water during modern wet-harvesting, since the water flows down from the top level to terraces below. The state's first bog, still bearing fruit, was planted by Cape Codder Charles Dexter McFarlin in 1885 in Coos County. He had gone west to seek his fortune in the California Gold Rush, failed, and turned to "red gold," ordering vines from Massachusetts and then developing a variety adapted to Oregon growing conditions. Oregon bogs tend to be small, under 10 acres. Yields average more than 100 barrels per acre.

Cranberries are also grown commercially in two widely separated parts of Canada. Most bogs are near Vancouver, British Columbia, on the Pacific coast, where cultivation was started in 1924, but some cranberries are also grown around Drummondville, Quebec, in the East. Canada has about 1200 acres planted with cranberries, and regularly accounts for 5 to 7 percent of the North American crop. One of its more unusual cranberry areas is on Lulu Island, British Columbia—it is below sea level and protected from the sea by dikes, like many parts of the Netherlands. The first bog was built there in 1932. Canadian bogs average a very high 135 barrels per acre.

Over the years, a number of mechanical devices have helped to increase yield and efficiency in the bogs. Washington growers pioneered the use of automatic sprinklers for irrigation and frost protection in the 1920s, and sprinklers are now widely used in all cranberry regions.

46

Cranberry harvesting picker, a rake-like wooden tool used in the early days and still well suited to the gathering of wild cranberries.

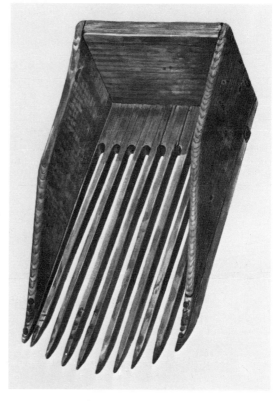

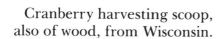

Cranberry harvesting scoop, also of wood, from Wisconsin.

Wet harvesting cranberries with water reels that beat the berries from the vines underwater. The berries float on the surface of the flooded bog until they are pushed to shore.

50

Wet harvesting is far more common and is even more efficient. Wisconsin growers were the first to use this method. "Raking on the flood" began to replace scooping in Wisconsin about 1920. With the bog flooded to a depth of about a foot, the vines with their floating berries rose to the surface, where the berries could be pulled away by large rakes equipped with long, curving teeth. Mechanization did not come along until 1943, when Wisconsin growers developed two types of picking machines.

The most common wet-pick method grew out of experiments in Oregon and the invention in 1948 of an early water reel by Sumner Fish. His "egg beater" had a ½-horsepower gasoline motor and a series of steel rods connected to wheels at either end. A worker simply walked the machine through the flooded bog and knocked the berries from the vines. It took about three hours to harvest the fruit from one acre of bog.

Today, big modern water reels ride in and churn up the water as the cranberries float like so many balloons on strings. The turbulence underwater dislodges the berries, which cover the surface of the water like a gorgeous ruby carpet. The loose berries, sometimes helped along by breezes and gentle currents, are corralled and pushed toward the shore. Workers in high rubber wading boots "boom" or "raft" the cranberries with the aid of floating hinged wooden slats (called "booms"). A truck parked close to the bog inserts a chute like a giant straw to pump and suck the berries out of the water. When one truck is filled, another drives up for more, running back and forth between bog and receiving station all day.

From Labor Day to first frost, harvest days are long and hectic—there are 14-hour days and no weekends off. Cranberries off the vine deteriorate quickly, and they must be processed or

Following two pages:
"Booming" cranberries after the water reels
have knocked them off the vines.

frozen within twenty-four hours. They arrive at the receiving stations in one of two ways: in bulk or by the box.

While most arrive in bulk in trucks, cranberries destined to be sold fresh arrive in wooden field boxes that hold only about 33 pounds each. This is high-quality fruit and must not be damaged or crushed! It is held in the boxes at cool temperatures, then moved quickly on conveyors to be separated from leaves, sticks, and stones that may have been picked up; "winnowing" blows away the trash. Then the berries must pass the "bounce test." They are

Cranberries taking the "bounce test" in the separator.

put through a machine called the separator, which forces each cranberry to hop over seven small wooden barriers or louvers. Seven chances to bounce like a basketball—and the cranberry that makes it joins other perfect berries. (A soft, rotten, or bruised berry simply has no bounce, and it lands in a bin with other rejects!) The good berries are then inspected by hand and eye by workers who pick out any unripe or imperfect fruit that may have sneaked by. The cranberries are then packed at high speed in small cartons or poly bags for shipment to market.

Cranberries headed for the canneries arrive in bulk; on arrival at the receiving station these will all be used eventually for sauce and juice drinks. As they are dumped to be weighed, a foreman takes a "cup count" to check the quality of the load. These berries too are cleaned. If it is a very busy day, they are temporarily placed in giant holding bins before, just hours away from the bogs, they undergo the bounce test. Most will be frozen for processing later on. Since freezing actually improves the juice output of cranberries, all fruit to be used for drinks spends at least four weeks in the freezer before being pressed.

There are now about 25,000 acres of cranberry bogs in North America, 20,000 of which are tended by members of Ocean Spray. Fresh cranberries account for only about 6 percent of total sales. The price of fresh cranberries goes up and down depending on the size of each year's crop. They are marketed from first harvest until New Year's. Ocean Spray members now produce about 85 percent of all cranberry products, most of which are canned, bottled, and frozen. Such year-round products include canned whole-berry and jellied sauce, relishes (with oranges and raspberries), and juice drinks, including blends with apple, grape, prune, and apricot juices. Low-calorie products are also sold. Cranberries are a good

Fresh cranberries being packaged for market
by a machine that forms, fills, cuts off, and seals
one poly bag after another.

source of vitamin C, but pure 100 percent cranberry juice (like lemon juice) is much too sour to drink plain. For bottling, it is diluted with water and sweetened to taste. Supplemental vitamin C is added, but the ruby red of the natural juice calls for no added coloring.

The cranberry, once a Cape Cod curiosity (and a bit too tart for many people's taste!) is now an all-American favorite. Cranberry products are enjoyed regularly in more than half of the households in the nation—not just at Thanksgiving!

Crane

Three Special Cranberry Places

Cape Cod National Seashore

Wild cranberries can be found in the lowlands near the Province Lands Visitors Center on Race Point Road, Provincetown. A small cultivated bog can be seen on the half-mile Cranberry Bog Trail, one of nine self-guided walking trails in the National Seashore, open year round. The Trail is accessible from Highway 6 at North Pamet Road, Truro. The Pamet bog, originally swampland, was cultivated in the 1880s but later fell into disuse. It was bought by the federal government in 1963 and a small cranberry patch was preserved to honor the heritage of the land.

Edaville Railroad

Off Route 58 in South Carver, Massachusetts, this old-fashioned train runs 5½ miles through cranberry bogs. Engine, steam cars, coaches, and freight cars are scaled to the narrow-gauge roadbed. It began as a working train that collected boxes of harvested berries from pickup points in the bogs, and was converted to a tourist excursion train in 1950. Open June through October and weekends in May. Admission is charged.

Cranberry World Visitors Center

On Water Street in Plymouth, a ten-minute walk from Plymouth Rock and the *Mayflower II*, this exhibit features outdoor working bogs, a scale-model cranberry farm, antique harvesting tools, twice-daily cooking demonstrations, demonstrations of how cranberry products are made, arts and crafts shows, and Sunday boardwalk concerts. Operated by Ocean Spray, the growers' cooperative. Open daily including holidays from April 1 to November 30. Admission and refreshments are free.

Cranberry Recipes

Blushing Apples (from an old Cape Cod cookbook)

Choose firm, tart baking apples and polish them. Remove the stems and cores but peel the skin down from the top only about an inch. Do not peel the rest of the apple. Put apples in a baking pan or dish and fill the cavities with cranberry jelly. Dot with butter. Pour water (or cranberry juice) around apples to a depth of ½ inch. Bake at 375 degrees for 30-40 minutes or until tender. Baste several times during cooking with the juices. Serve warm or cold, with cream.

Wild-Cranberry Sauce (Pond Island, Maine)
2 cups wild cranberries, including a few underripe ones for pectin
1 cup sugar
½ cup water

Combine all ingredients in a saucepan and cook over low heat, stirring now and then, until berries pop. This should not take more than 10 minutes. Cool.

Cranberry Yogurt

Stir whole-berry cranberry sauce into plain or vanilla yogurt. The plain will be very tart, but the vanilla will be sweet. Or use the plain and add a little sugar to your taste.

Quick Chutney for Poultry (Courtesy of the Ocean Spray Kitchen at the Cranberry World Visitors Center)

Combine 1 can whole-berry cranberry sauce with ½ cup raisins and ½ cup chopped pear or peach. Add ½ teaspoon ground ginger. Chill for several hours.

To Keep Fresh Cranberries for Up to a Year:

For store-bought (cultivated) cranberries: follow directions on bag or box— simply put, as is, in the freezer.

For wild cranberries: pick over berries for bits of trash, wash them well in cold water. Discard any berries that are soft. Pack dry in airtight containers such as jars or noncrushable plastic boxes. Freeze.

Cranberry Cake (Pond Island, Maine)
⅓ cup butter
2 eggs
milk
2 tsp. baking powder
½ tsp. salt
2 (scant) cups flour
1 tsp. vanilla extract
1 cup fresh cranberries, coarsely chopped
1 cup sugar, plus 1 tbsp.

Sprinkle 1 tbsp. sugar over chopped cranberries. Melt butter over low heat in measuring cup—do not burn. When cool, break in eggs and fill cup with milk. Put in bowl. Sift dry ingredients and add to egg mixture while beating. Add vanilla and fold in cranberries. Bake in loaf pan at 375°F. for about 40-45 minutes. This cake can also be baked in an 8 × 8-inch pan, which will take less baking time.

Cranberry-Raisin Stuffing (for Chicken or Turkey)
⅔ cup chopped fresh cranberries (or more)
2 tbsp. sugar
pinch of salt
about 3 cups cubes made from stale raisin bread
2 tbsp. butter or margarine, melted
¼ cup orange juice
grated orange peel (if desired), about 1-2 tsp.

Combine cranberries, sugar, salt, and orange peel. Toss with bread cubes. Sprinkle melted butter and orange juice over cubes and mix lightly. Bake in a casserole, covered, for about 45 minutes at 325-350°F. (If your raisin bread is fresh, cut the cubes and leave them overnight to dry out.)

Cranberry Varieties

While there are more than 100 varieties today, just four of these account for most of the North American commercial crop:

Early Black

By far the most common; standard in Massachusetts and New Jersey. It is small, ripens as early as late August, is very deep red (almost black), has fine flavor, and is a good keeper. Sold fresh; dark color is good for juicing. First cultivated about 1850 in Harwich on Cape Cod, it is not a developed variety but a direct descendant of the wild Cape Cod cranberry.

McFarlin

Principal variety in Washington and Oregon, also widely grown in Wisconsin and Canada. It is nearly oblong, dark red, and ripens late. Named for the first commercial grower on the West coast, it was developed from Massachusetts vines.

Searles

Grown mainly in Wisconsin. Its berries are deep red and ripen in midseason (late September). It was first grown near Wisconsin Rapids in 1894 by Andrew Searles.

Howes

The standard "late" cranberry, grown primarily in Massachusetts and New Jersey. It was first grown in 1843 by Eli Howes of East Dennis, Cape Cod. It is oblong, medium red, and larger than the Early Black. High in pectin, it makes good jelly and sauce and is also sold fresh. Early Black and Howes together are grown more than all other varieties.

Index